Nancy Lopez
Super Golfer

by Janet Woodward

Harcourt
SCHOOL PUBLISHERS

3, 10, 11 ©Corbis; 4–9 Chantal Stewart ©Harcourt Education Australia; 12–14 ©Getty Images

Printed in the United States of America

ISBN 10: 0-15-350404-8
ISBN 13: 978-0-15-350404-4

Ordering Options
ISBN 10: 0-15-350332-7 (Grade 2 Below-Level Collection)
ISBN 13: 978-0-15-350332-0 (Grade 2 Below-Level Collection)
ISBN 10: 0-15-357431-3 (package of 5)
ISBN 13: 978-0-15-357431-3 (package of 5)

1 2 3 4 5 6 7 8 9 10   179   15 14 13 12 11 10 09 08 07 06

Nancy Lopez was a top golf player.

Some top players begin because a brother or sister plays golf.

Nancy caught her love of golf as a child. Her parents played the game. She would follow them around the course.

When she was eight, her dad
helped her learn to play.

He made a sand trap in their yard. After school, Nancy would go straight outside and work on her golf.

Nancy had her first win when she was nine. At twelve, she came in first in an important golf contest. The people watching gave a big cheer.

There was no girls' golf team at Nancy's high school. Nancy tried playing for the boys' team. With Nancy playing, the boys' team could not lose!

In 1977, Nancy started
making money playing golf.

She became a true golf star.
She finished first in many
contests.

Nancy was named "Player of the Year" three times.

In 1997, she played in her
last big golf contest. She hit
fewer shots each day than any
woman ever had.

Today Nancy is a mother and
runs her own golf company.

Think Critically

1. How old was Nancy when she had her first win?

2. How can you tell that this book is nonfiction?

3. What are two words that you would use to tell about Nancy Lopez?

4. Did you think Nancy would keep playing golf when she finished high school?

5. Would you like to play golf? Why or why not?

 **Social Studies**

Make a Storyboard Make a storyboard of the important events in Nancy's golfing career. Draw a picture of each part of her career. Write a sentence under each picture.

School-Home Connection Talk about the book with a family member. Then talk about why it is important to practice things that are difficult to do.

Word Count: 188